THE
PRESENT
FROM
Aunt Skidoo

Joshua was not the least surprised when he didn't get a birthday present from his Aunt Skidoo. He knew in his bones it would turn up sooner or later. It always did.

In fact, for every birthday that Joshua could remember, Aunt Skidoo had sent him handkerchiefs. So you can understand why he didn't rise up in a froth of excitement when his mother called, "Joshua, dear, here's a very late present from Aunt Skidoo."

"Terrific," said Joshua. "I'll put them in my top drawer with all the other ones."

"Now, Joshua dear, don't be so unkind. It's the thought that counts," said his mother, as she dragged his present into the room.

"Wow!" said Joshua. "This present is big. It has edges and sharp points. It looks interesting! This doesn't look like handkerchiefs!"

The paper peeled off like a snake's skin, and inside was indeed a most wonderful present. Well, at least it wasn't handkerchiefs.

There was only one small problem. Joshua couldn't tell what it was. It seemed to be a bundle of sticks, a ball of string, and a big piece of red material.

"Whatever is it?" said Joshua. Then under the sticks he found a crumpled envelope. Inside was a letter. He could just make out the words *Dear Joshua... a fly-away notion...*

5

"A fly-away notion," Joshua murmured to himself, as he looked doubtfully at the sticks and the material. "This doesn't look like it could fly away. Hmmmm! If I just twist this here...and twist that there... and tie this piece of string around that..."

Joshua's new kite floated gently into the air and then suddenly gathered speed, until it flew in great whirling loops like a big red insect menacing the clouds for miles around.

Oak Road
reenwoods
Monday

Dear Aunt Skidoo,

Thank you very much for my birthday kite. It is more than a fly-away notion. It is a sky-flying monster. It zoomed down onto our roof at the speed of light and gave a flock of gulls sitting up there a very nasty fright. In fact, Dad is still up there, trying to untangle the kite from the chimney.

With lots of love from your nephew,

Joshua

A few days later, a letter arrived for Joshua.

Dear Joshua,

My dear boy, I'm very confused about your birthday present. I didn't send you a kite.

Your loving Aunt Skidoo

"If it's not a kite...what is it?" thought Joshua. He found his aunt's letter. "The trouble is," said Joshua, "this letter is too crumpled to read." With the aid of a large magnifying glass, he made out the word *shelter.* He eyed the poles and the red material.

"If that's a shelter, then I'm a green elephant," said his father.

But Joshua already had his building under way. "Can't you see, Dad? It's a tent. That's a kind of shelter. Now why didn't I think of that before?"

Joshua and his pals gathered in the tent. They planned hunting trips on nearby moose, they toasted marshmallows on sticks, they huddled inside when it rained.

Oak Road

eenwoods

Sunday

Dear Aunt Skidoo,

Thank you very much for the tent. It works well as a shelter, not only from the rain, but also from Grandpa when he comes looking for his chickens. I don't think he understands that in the excitement of a hunt it's very difficult to tell the difference between a chicken and a moose.

Bye for now,

Joshua

In a few days, another letter arrived for Joshua.

Dear Joshua,
How can such a simple birthday present cause such problems? What's this about a tent?

Your loving Aunt Skidoo

Once more, Joshua examined the writing on his birthday letter. "This looks like... I think it's...*trap*. Yes, that's it."

Joshua's face lit up like a lighthouse. "This is too good to be true," he thought. "A trap is exactly what we need around here. We are overrun with wild animals. It just isn't safe to walk around anymore. You never know when you might feel hot breath and lion's teeth a bit too close for comfort." His neck felt all prickly at the thought.

15

Joshua spent all afternoon digging a big hole and rigging up the sticks and the material. At dusk – lion-feeding time – he hid very quietly in the bushes and watched his trap through a pair of binoculars.

...ak Road

...enwoods

...turday

Dear Aunt Skidoo,

Thank you for the great trap you sent me. It works extremely well. I didn't have much luck at first. In fact, I nearly fell asleep. No chance of a snooze, though, once I had a lion trapped. The roars were bloodcurdling. A shame it was only Dad. You would think an experienced hunter like Dad wouldn't have made such a simple mistake!

Take care,

Joshua

The next week, another letter arrived.

Dear Joshua,

I'm speechless. How you ever caught your father with my birthday present is beyond me!

Your loving Aunt Skidoo

Joshua was puzzled. He took out the birthday letter again. He looked long and hard at the faded blue ink and crumpled paper. "I think it says *lip* and *lide*," he said.

"Well, that doesn't make much sense," said his father huffily. He'd had quite enough of Joshua's birthday present.

Joshua stuck the piece of paper to the window and then looked at it through binoculars. Now he could read the words *slip* and *slide*. He was almost speechless with delight.

19

"This is unbelievable! Aunt Skidoo must be able to read my mind. She has sent me a mud-slider."

Joshua poured water down the bank until the thick mud glistened like oil. Then he carefully lowered himself onto the mud-slider, adjusted the poles, and closed his eyes. With an ear-piercing "Mud awaaaay!" he slid at breakneck speed to the bottom of the slide, where he lay covered in mud and completely contented.

"Joshua," called his mother, "look who's here. We have a visitor. It's your Aunt Skidoo."

"Joshua, dear boy. Is that you under all that mud?" said Aunt Skidoo. "Whatever do you think of me? To think I sent you all those letters and you never got your present."

21

"I realized when this package came to me that it should have gone to you." Aunt Skidoo stopped and peered at Joshua's mud-slider. "So THAT'S where those got to!"

"Now I see what happened. The store sent you my new bean poles and leaf-catcher along with the letter I'd left for you. No wonder you couldn't make sense of it. What a wonderful surprise I have for you! Happy birthday, dear boy."

She pushed a small package and letter into Joshua's hands. Joshua opened the birthday letter. This time it was easy to read. He whispered the lines slowly to himself.

6 First Avenue
Pinehaven
Wednesday

Dear Joshua,

It's never a fly-away notion
To have one floating around
Because when you're feeling ill
Or need shelter from a chill
Simply slip one in your pocket
Or slide one up your sleeve.
There's no better way
To trap a runaway sneeze
So you really must have
At least one or two of
these.

Your loving Aunt Skidoo

"Don't tell me," said Joshua. "No, please, let me guess. It's some handkerchiefs."